The
Digestive
System

by Rebecca Pettiford

Note to Librarians, Teachers, and Parents:

Blastoff! Readers are carefully developed by literacy experts and combine standards-based content with developmentally appropriate text.

Level 1 provides the most support through repetition of high-frequency words, light text, predictable sentence patterns, and strong visual support.

Level 2 offers early readers a bit more challenge through varied simple sentences, increased text load, and less repetition of high-frequency words.

Level 3 advances early-fluent readers toward fluency through increased text and concept load, less reliance on visuals, longer sentences, and more literary language.

Level 4 builds reading stamina by providing more text per page, increased use of punctuation, greater variation in sentence patterns, and increasingly challenging vocabulary.

Level 5 encourages children to move from "learning to read" to "reading to learn" by providing even more text, varied writing styles, and less familiar topics.

Whichever book is right for your reader, Blastoff! Readers are the perfect books to build confidence and encourage a love of reading that will last a lifetime!

This edition first published in 2020 by Bellwether Media, Inc.

No part of this publication may be reproduced in whole or in part without written permission of the publisher. For information regarding permission, write to Bellwether Media, Inc., Attention: Permissions Department, 6012 Blue Circle Drive, Minnetonka, MN 55343.

Library of Congress Cataloging-in-Publication Data

Names: Pettiford, Rebecca, author.
Title: The Digestive System / by Rebecca Pettiford.
Description: Minneapolis, MN : Bellwether Media, Inc., 2020. | Series: Blastoff! Readers. Your Body Systems | Audience: Ages 5-8. | Audience: K to grade 3. | Includes bibliographical references and index.
Identifiers: LCCN 2018056078 (print) | LCCN 2018057530 (ebook) | ISBN 9781618915603 (ebook) | ISBN 9781644870198 (hardcover : alk. paper) | ISBN 9781618917522 (pbk. : alk. paper)
Subjects: LCSH: Digestive–Juvenile literature. | Gastrointestinal system–Physiology–Juvenile literature.
Classification: LCC QP145 (ebook) | LCC QP145 .P458 2020 (print) | DDC 612.3–dc23
LC record available at https://lccn.loc.gov/2018056078

Table of Contents

What Is the Digestive System?

The human body runs on **nutrients**. Nutrients come from the food we eat.

The digestive system is a group of **organs**. These organs work together to change food into nutrients. This system also removes waste.

The digestive system is about 30 feet (9 meters) long! All the food we eat passes through it.

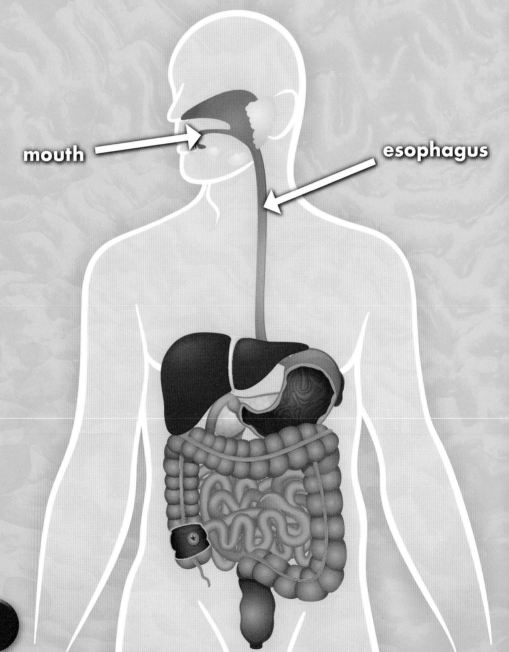

mouth

esophagus

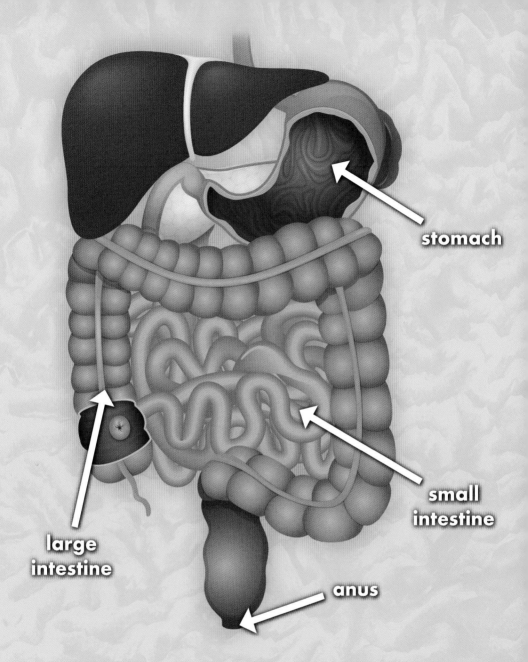

stomach

small
intestine

large
intestine

anus

It includes the mouth, esophagus,
and stomach. It also includes
the small and large intestines,
and the anus.

How Does the Digestive System Work?

Digestion begins in the mouth. Food gets broken down when it is chewed.

The mouth makes **saliva**.
It is filled with **enzymes** that
break down food. Saliva also
makes food wet. This makes
food easier to swallow.

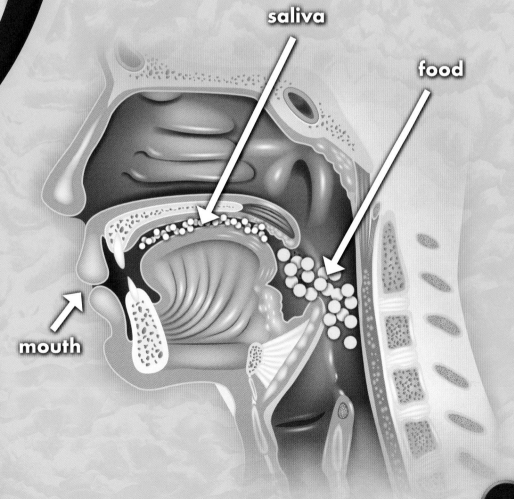

saliva

food

mouth

Food enters a long tube called the esophagus. **Muscles** in the tube push food into the stomach.

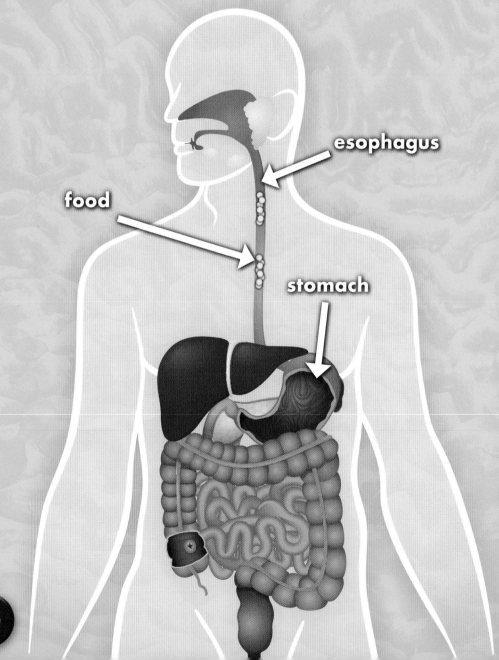

esophagus

food

stomach

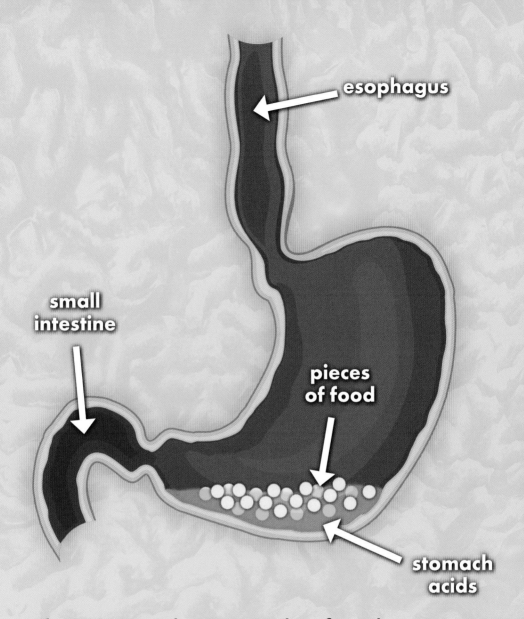

esophagus

small intestine

pieces of food

stomach acids

The stomach mixes the food with **acids**. This breaks the food down even more! Then the food passes into the **small intestine**.

Other organs go to work!
The **pancreas** releases enzymes.
They break down the food, too.

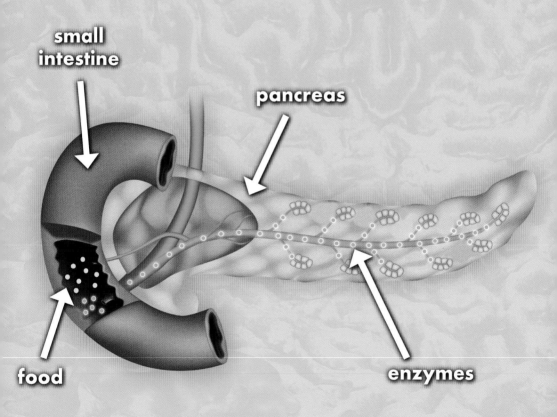

small
intestine

pancreas

food

enzymes

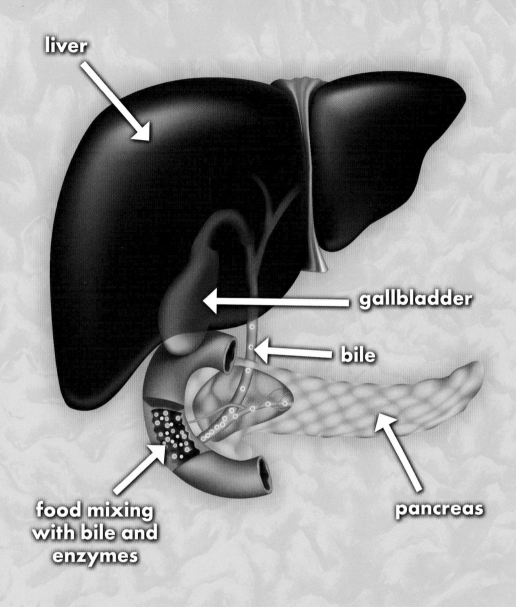

liver

gallbladder

bile

food mixing with bile and enzymes

pancreas

Bile from the **liver** moves into the **gallbladder**. The gallbladder releases bile into the small intestine to break down fats.

Villi line the walls of the small intestine where they collect nutrients. They look like tiny fingers!

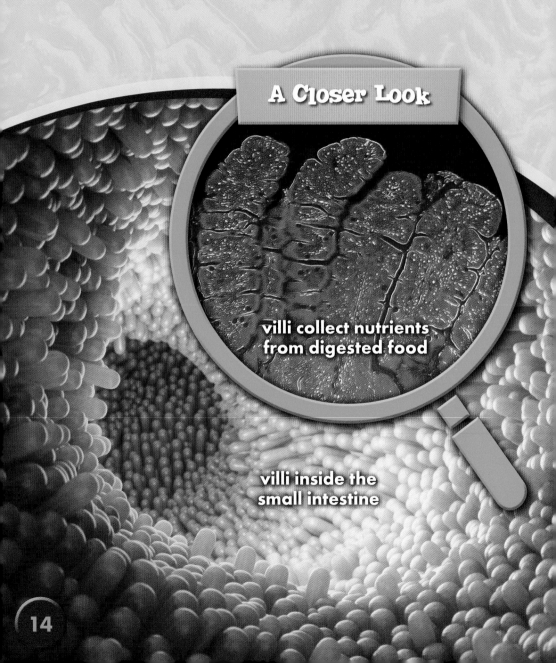

A Closer Look

villi collect nutrients from digested food

villi inside the small intestine

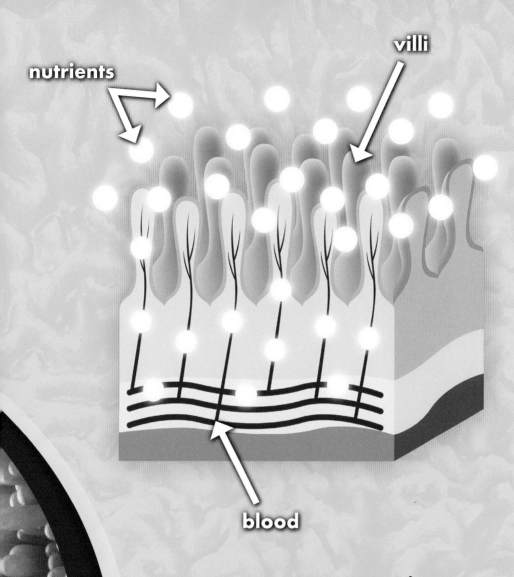

nutrients

villi

blood

Nutrients enter the blood through the villi. The blood carries the nutrients through the body.

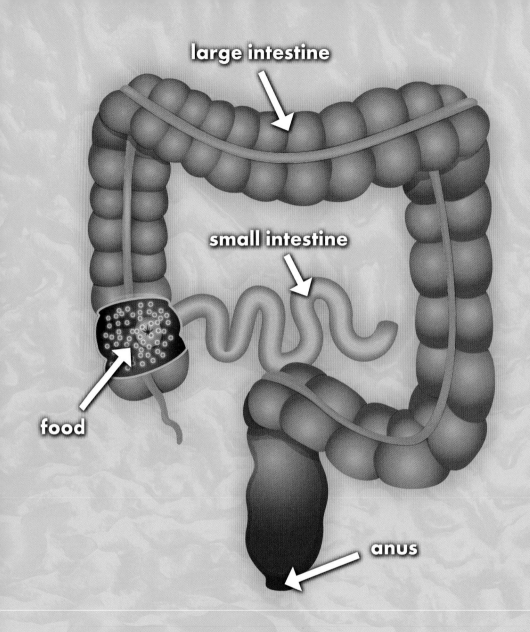

large intestine

small intestine

food

anus

The food that remains moves to the **large intestine**. Some water moves there, too. The large intestine removes the water.

Solid waste is left. It leaves the body through the anus.

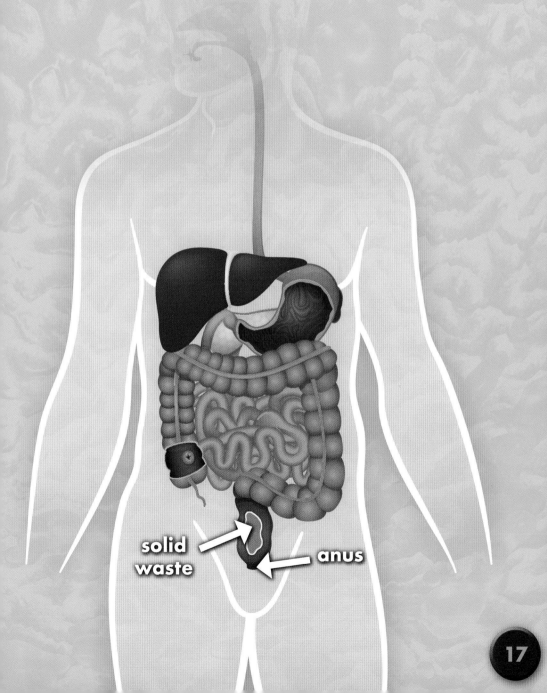

solid waste

anus

Why Is the Digestive System Important?

The nutrients we get from food give us **energy**. We use energy to learn. We use it to work. We use it to play sports!

Your Digestive System at Work!

See what happens to food when the stomach mixes it and breaks it down.

You will need:
- one piece of bread
- 3 tablespoons of water
- one sealable plastic bag

1. Put the piece of bread and the water in the plastic bag. Seal the bag.

2. Use your hands to squeeze the bag to mix the bread and water. This is like the stomach mixing food with stomach acids.

3. Notice how mixing the bread with the water (stomach acids) turns the bread into a soupy mix. This is like the food in your stomach!

Eating a balanced diet and drinking water keeps the digestive system healthy.

The next time you eat, you will know what is happening to your food!

Glossary

acids—liquids that break down food

bile—a thick, greenish liquid made by the liver that helps the body digest fats

energy—the power to move and do things

enzymes—substances that help digestion

gallbladder—an organ that stores bile

large intestine—the tube-shaped organ that removes water from food to form waste

liver—a large organ that makes bile and cleans the blood

muscles—body tissues that help move parts of the body

nutrients—the things humans need to live and grow

organs—parts of the body that have a special job

pancreas—a large organ that makes enzymes that help digest food

saliva—a watery liquid in the mouth that makes food wet; saliva has enzymes that break down food.

small intestine—the long, tube-shaped organ where food is digested after it leaves the stomach; the small intestine is where nutrients enter the blood.

villi—fingerlike parts of the small intestine that move nutrients into the blood

To Learn More

AT THE LIBRARY
Kenney, Karen Latchana. *Digestive System*. Minneapolis, Minn.: Jump!, 2017.

Mahoney, Emily. *20 Fun Facts about the Digestive System*. New York, N.Y.: Gareth Stevens Publishing, 2019.

Sohn, Emily. *A Journey Through the Digestive System with Max Axiom, Super Scientist: 4D An Augmented Reading Science Experience*. North Mankato, Minn.: Capstone Press, 2019.

ON THE WEB

FACTSURFER

Factsurfer.com gives you a safe, fun way to find more information.

1. Go to www.factsurfer.com.

2. Enter "digestive system" into the search box and click Q.

3. Select your book cover to see a list of related web sites.

Index

The images in this book are reproduced through the courtesy of: mdgraphcs, front cover; Ermolaev Alexander, p. 4; margouillat photo, p. 5; Marochkina Anastasiia, pp. 6-7, 10, 16, 17; Teguh Mujiono, p. 8; Pressmaster, p. 9; logika600, p. 11; Alila Medical Media, pp. 12, 13; Kateryna Kon, p. 14 (top); Rost9, p. 14 (bottom); gritsalak karalak, p. 15; Sergey Novikov, p. 18; Yellow Cat, p. 19 (left); Seregam, p. 19 (middle); Coprid, p. 19 (right); hanapon1002, p. 20; TairA, p. 21.